Unknown Depths

Nichole Pientka

BookLeaf Publishing

India | USA | UK

Presentation by *BookLeaf Publishing*

Web: www.bookleafpub.com

E-mail: info@bookleafpub.com

ISBN: 9789358315370

First edition 2023

*Dedicated to my partner, John Bonadurer IV,
my family, and my friends who have supported
and nurtured me as a person and writer.*

ACKNOWLEDGEMENT

First, I'd like to thank my sixth-grade teacher, Mrs. Janice McArdle,—may she rest in peace—for encouraging my writing at an early age. I'd also like to thank my concurrent members of Writehouse Ink. at Bradley University for their dedication to writing and for helping me evolve as a writer as well as my professors, Drs. Kevin Stein and Devin Murphy, for their professional writing advice and guidance.

PREFACE

This collection of poems is inspired by and reflects my experiences in this ever-changing world of finding fulfillment, love, death, and causes worth believing in.

Hands Shaping Love

You can tell a lot by a person's hands.
My hands, I'm told are my father's:
Long fingers and nail beds,
double-jointed thumbs.
Maybe they are the same as my grandfather's
Made for shaping clay,
forming vessels of his love,

Creating objects from gray matter
like my mind composes verses.
He gifted me a mug in December,
became my favorite once I saw it
Slate blue with speckles and a unique handle
like strings on a violin,
Short and perfect for cappuccinos, lattes, tea.

I was drinking out of it when I heard
the grim news staring through the dregs
of espresso and oat milk,
I knew his initials were there.
Same as my father and uncle's.

I wish the mug was full again, warm again.
It will be painful to be reminded of him,
of how he won't make another like it.

The short, blue mug is special, like he was.
His clay creations weren't perfect;

Neither was he, but his intentions were good,
hopeful, loving. I was looking forward to
having him and Val over to our house
in the summer, but at least I saw him
days before Christmas.
I will hold that blessing with me

I will heed his advice
about the tall, wonky front step—
Needs to be removed and replaced
with a new one—
And we'll pour that concrete with the love
Grandpa had for us.

Nightmare

Convinced she's awake
Spider crawling into bed
Pounding heart, gasping,
Watching the scene unfold
From above and within her
Body springing up, out,
Away until her consciousness
Alights with a lamp switched on
Shadows of her mind abated
For now

Dear Uncle Jeff

Your pain never ends
Denial, oxy, money
Only degrades you

Homeless, paranoid,
Manipulating, and poor
Second-hand stories

Your addicted mind
Doesn't see you've hit bottom
Dark and desperate

Healing

5

They thought prayers would heal
anything if praying hard, long enough.
Couldn't heal family ties, bonds:
estranged youngest sons, addiction,
misjudgment, divorces, illness, cancer.

Prayer has power, but only if willing
to heal yourself, apologize, love
without reservation. It comes from within
before it can help others.

Goodbye

Absence stings like a mosquito bite
Onset is quick, needle, drawing blood
No dripping, leaving nothing behind
Except
Leaving
Venom deep until
Swollen, red, blotch blooms
Minutes, hours, a day later
Itch
Itch
Itching skin deep
Muscle memory
Triggered by something scratched
A record, melody, buzzing static
Buzzing around your head
Memory picked raw, scabbed over
Itch
Itch scratch buried and healed over
Time, knitting skin, disconnecting neurons
Until the itch comes back
Forefront, head, brain, straight to heart

Three Dots

7

He speaks in ellipsis…
Three dots separating him from you…
His engineer brain is wired differently…
Fast synapses, missing clues…
Facial cues eclipsed, omitted…
Too many incomplete thoughts…
Like the menu on smartphones…
There's more to what he's saying…
But you have to press…

Traveling Taste Buds

When our friends cook
traditional Chinese meals,
we don't eat until past 8 p.m.
Facing heaven, red thai, serrano
peppers fragrance the house,
burning sinuses, opening windows.
We leave with bellies full of memories,
burning lips eager to quench our thirst,
inspiration to expand our palates, and ready
for our taste buds to travel to far off places.

It Can't All Be Kitsch

He says he can't help listening
to lashes sweeping her pillowcase as she wakes.
Her open eyes are lost
Morpho butterfly wings dangling on earlobes,
stolen souvenirs from rainforest mist.
He waits as she blinks promises
without meaning to.

He wants to open her seafoam petals.

She answers, Romans lured Venus
with fermented fruit to display her
on mantels, concealing her love
for their own pleasure.

He declares her curves remind him
of goddess Nike designed in truth
and marble. She flinches
as he traces knobs of her spine,
between her shoulder blades, where
wings would be.

She lands in his palms once more,
no longer denying him. He sups
from rubied lips, paying homage

to her spirit for his spoils.
She laments the pearl, now a silver scar,
once formed within her skull
and stored in her second chakra.

He believes Adonis' death a hunting accident
not revenge; fate ruled by nature. She shakes
her head. Venus scattered his blood
where anemones sprout,
lapping up golden syrup.
Too sweet to spawn jealousy,
or at least too naïve.

She knows beauty only happens once.

Marionette

Sleet slashes panes of her fractured mind,
Her insides hum like plucked strings, quivering
with tension. Can't find the right note
to neutralize sensations growing
stronger by the second
defense of colored capsules and slumber.
Blank, boring her eyes into the wall,
she attempts to go numb. She feels too much.

It's her nature, biology; something locked
beneath skin others cannot comprehend.
She's a mirage, seen through mind's eye
as complete. In reality; remnants
of smoke and mirrors
leaving her stranded and incorporeal.

She hangs in dusty air among snowy particles,
unclear even in sunlight,
then hiding in cool confinement.
Tears on her lips, screaming from her eyes,
gravity heaves her toward Earth with each tread
by a steel cable running from skull to feet.

Shadows tethered to concrete:
a marionette too aware of her body.

Distance from Buildings
Doesn't Matter

Staggering down sidewalk
along red-bricked strip mall,
determined to get my fix,
gaggles of giggling freshmen
shuffle toward and disperse 'round me.
Heavy-lidded eyes catch my reflection
lit by red and blue neon OPEN sign:
transparent image of woman
with ochre skin dappled by scars and freckles,
unlit cigarette hanging from gashed mouth
like extra appendage dangling in twilit breeze.

I was beautiful once.

Hobbling in hip pain
from wiping out on ice in size-four graying
off-brand jeans and faded black shirt
stolen from Salvation Army bin.
Left arm still stays akimbo on
good leg's side for balance.
Hip pain's not as bad as my craving
for my one last cigarette to be lit, but
I'm fuckin' outta matches.
Approach another group of preppy students,

almost unable to speak, needy.
I try rasping, "Yuhavefire?"
Girls avoid my question by stepping off
drying cement onto the soggy street.
Tobacco: nothing else matters:
my gritty tongue longs for it,
organs call out like sirens.
My veined eyes plead passersby
for lighter, already smoking butt.
I feel half-dead, zombie:
Voodoo kind my Haitian
ancestors believed real
dark magic won't restore me.
I slink past packed Starbucks
toward Jimmy's local bar and grill.

Hint of cigarette smoke
diffuses in my lungs near outdoor tables.
My mission fulfilled by fellow smokers
sitting legal distance from entrance.
Not bothering to form words,
metallic click reveals lively flame.
Nostrils flaring, sunken eyes drift closed,
posture slumps bonelessly
against black metal fence.
I curl 'round my desired prize.
Trying not to think I'll be satisfied
till the ash sifts between
arthritic trembling fingers,

desperate itch will return
like fleas won't die.
The need will kill me.
It'll smite blonde stranger
armed with lighter, his eyes glazed.
So handsome now, but
he'll dissolve into addiction,
self-imposed ugly torture.
Deadly habit coats lungs and mouths
in cancer, brains want more.
Not smart after all.

Wondering

My finger next to my pinky
Left hand floating
Lonely, unadorned like
Nine other digits. Can it feel age?
Like my partner is mine without
Forget me Celtic knot tied around
Eight years braided together.
No papers, scrawled signatures,
Vows, rings, champagne
In my brain fizzles over when
The question about popping
The question, walking down the aisle
Pours out of mouths left and right.
Depends... until
He asks if I want to marry him
Some day. My stomach flips like
During our first kiss and "I love you"
And I say, "Yes, of course"
Tears and a smile line his face.

A Dog's Life

Is pretty simple:
Tail wags, treats, table scraps,
Scratches behind the ears,
Muddy paw prints, lots of licks,
Wet noses, chasing squirrels,
Long walks around neighborhood,
Sniffing safaris, cuddles in bed,
Tummy rubs, playing fetch,
Pitty smiles, squeaking toys,
And a lifetime of love.

Seasoning Greetings Recipe

Yield: 12 hectic days of Christmas
Prep Time: Longer than you think

Ingredients:
16 cups of blended time,* maybe a dash(er) here
or there more
Includes: 1 Christian holy day + 8 days of
Hanukkah + 7 days of Kwanzaa
5 strings of partially-working lights (assorted)
1 assembled pre-lit artificial tree
25 mini bottles of wine in an advent calendar
$500 in spare change
3 bins of dusty ornaments
5 burning candles smelling like holiday spirits
60 hours of upbeat, whining, holiday music
blaring in grocery and retail stores
20 times of checking your list, checking it twice
4 rolls of wrapping paper and 2 tape dispensers
1 lost pair of scissors
1 headache induced by wrapping presents
(and maybe the wine)
7 last-minute stocking stuffers
3 half-eaten frosted snowman-shaped sugar
cookies
Mid-morning dusting of snow on Christmas Eve

Instructions:
1. First, don't put the elf on the shelf and make sure Rudolph's nose isn't blinding neighbors.
2. Your calendar must be full. There is no downtime, no wiggle room for naps, sugar comas, or hangovers. Measure exactly!
3. Add your dollars upfront for gifts, the earlier the better. Even in November, you won't miss those popular and classic holiday tunes at all the stores. Bring your list!
4. The tree goes up as soon as the turkey leftovers are in the fridge, no exceptions! Hang those lights that same day and be careful hanging those fragile ornaments.
5. Combine wrapping paper, tape, and scissors (if you can find them).
6. Light those candles during your wrapping sessions after work and be sure to crack open each bottle of wine until Christmas. Keep Excedrin on hand for headaches.
7. Stuff the stockings until full and decide whether or not to polish off those cookies.
8. Debate on putting out salt on the sidewalk for visitors.

Recipe Notes: *Can't have too much time, really. There's never enough!

Obligation

A fine line exists between
Obligation and love:
If you love someone, it's not
obligatory. Except sometimes–
you must part with your soul,
true desires, sacrifice pieces of
sanity until there are more cracks
than wholeness.

Transactions come easily,
but they're hollow when blood
ties us together. Generational
Abuse: when the Elders expect
the youth to want something they don't.
Let them be, learn from the new world,
create holistic needs, bring us closer
rather than competing for people-pleasing
trophies and meaningless praise.

Because you had to fight for it, doesn't
mean that others should too. Pave the way
for others to gain equality, equity, happiness,
a good life. Work to live or live to work,
choose your path but don't put up roadblocks
to the opposing viewpoint. Make satisfaction

reflect empathy instead of emptiness leading
to jealousy, animosity, and hate.

Strive to be the example
of love without obligation.

Charmed for the Holidays

21

If I could stop time, I'd have five holidays;
one for each facet of my life: Mom, Dad, sister,
friends, and partner's' families.
Or if I could be in multiple places at once,
I'd celebrate with all at the same time,
stretching my love, attention, and wallet.
It'd be worth it to not overplan, disappoint,
and exhaust myself and inner resources.
If I could see the future, I could predict when
Dad wanted to have a last-minute party or
when Mom comes into town. I could avoid
all blunders of holidays passed
if I were charmed.

Unknown Depths

22

With the dark waters of Loch Ness around us,
'Since we're in your favorite place,' he started,
'I wanted to ask: Would you want to get married
Some day? I'm not officially asking, but…'
"Yes, of course," I said. He smiled, blinking
Tears of joy down the curves of his cheeks.
It never occurred to me that he didn't know
How much I loved him, wanted him to be mine.
I didn't need Scotch to feel the warmth pooling
In my center, heart beating faster, while cruising
Over unknown depths with our future secure.

Prime Day Goes Postal

23

Another package on the porch
Barcodes, smiles, same addresses
Delivery trucks blocking intersections
Dogs barking at every paltry parcel

Recycling wedged full with cardboard origami
Worse than after Christmas morning
Collecting boxes becomes the norm
How many deliveries at your door?

How to Survive Commuting by Train

Step one: fill your backpack
with laptop, lunch, snacks, book
essentials like earbuds and coffee.
Don't bring more than one big bag
Or you risk lugging it upstairs or in aisle.

Step two: buy reusable, leak proof thermos
for coffee and tea. Fill it at home or
with latte bought at local shop since
disposable cups are likely to spill.
Bonus: it'll keep your beverage warm or cold!

Step three: learn boarding patterns
to find train car with the most vacant seats.
Express trains fill up quickly and might take
several days to scope it out. Don't be afraid
to sit next to someone and don't
Leave your bag on the seat when crowded.

We're all in this miserable commute together!

Step four: dress for the weather and in layers.
You may wait at least 10 minutes outside,
unsheltered in heat, wind, rain, or snow.

Keep umbrella, hat and gloves in bag,
and wear boots or gym shoes and bring
or keep dress shoes at the office.

Step five: enjoy the ride and look out
for announcements and delays.
Trains can be unpredictable!

Forehead Wrinkles

Spying smooth skin between brows
and hairline on others makes frown
lines deepen on my face when
I look in the mirror. I see all
the times I've raised, furrowed
my eyebrows, concentrated, laughed,
cried, squinted, questioned, expressed
myself in thirty years.

Are these other people expressionless?
Is it Botox injections or fancy skincare?
Anti-wrinkle massages? Red light therapy?
Some TikTok fad I've never seen?
I tried Frownies, but I couldn't sleep
with a plastered, stiff face.

Wrinkles are symptoms of aging,
wisdom lives in these life lines,
and I'll try to accept they're part of me.

PhANToms

The ants of the earth came knocking
for asylum. Well, they didn't knock, per se.
Ants marched through the cracks like
viruses squeezing through barriers
of flesh. They came to escape April showers,
for the crumbs we could spare. I could use Raid
like hand sanitizer and they'd still persist
drunkenly stumbling up my arms,
taking residence in garbage bags.
My skin crawls, oversensitized
by the bugs; legs skittering, antennae wiggling,
a fallen hair tickling the follicles of my leg.
A phantom sensation like goosebumps
I can't shake even if I think they're gone,
even if I know they won't kill me, harm me.
The minuscule, strong creatures will haunt
wallpaper, carpet, windowsills, cabinets,
my itching scalp, dry toes, cracked elbows.
I don't think they'll leave easily,
not from my mind at least,
where they are unwelcome squatters.
My body, my house is an ant farm
waiting for them to find another picnic.

Whisper

It starts with a whisper
A ripple of gooseflesh
Extra layers and raking leaves
Time to settle down, slowly
Embrace and brace for calm
For thanks, celebration, family